14 Years of a Life Sentence

"JOHN WILLIAM HURST"

ANNE SKINNER

DEDICATION

This book is dedicated to my friend
John William Hurst.
Praying that one day he will have his freedom again.

INTRODUCTION

For a long time now I have been writing to Mr. John William Hurst, I have found him to be sincere in all that he talks about.

Being many years in Ministry there have been many men and woman who have been incarcerated and yet there just didn't seem like the evidence was truly there to convict them of the crime. The sentences always seemed so harsh and I began to think that just maybe the system was like a warehousing operation where men and woman were put to just get them out of the way.

My heart goes out to these people like John who never had a fair chance, never had a good lawyer and now sitting year after year never have people who truly care.

I ask as you read this story that you stop tonight when you go to sleep and say a prayer for John and the millions of others behind bars.

They have a story to tell and it is only by God's grace that we are not in their shoes.

Rev. Anne Skinner

Nothing Is Impossible With God

GIVE UP

It's hard to wake up every morning, in this
same old place and ugly cage.
It's hard to get along with these people full of
rage.
It's hard to think ahead when the clocks
moving slow.
It's hard to have so many questions with
answers I don't know.
It's hard to think I'm smart when I lost
everything so fast,
It's hard to think about the future when I'm
stuck in the past.
It's hard to feel love when family has passed
away
It's hard to forget about mistakes when they left
so many scars.
It's hard to just move on when in life I have no
role
It's hard to have good dreams when my life's
depending on parole.
With everything being so hard,
You would think I'd just give up
But the thing about being at the bottom is that
the only way is UP!

By John William Hurst 2013

HERE IS MY STORY

My name is John William Hurst, I am an innocent man doing life in a Texas Prison.

I was born on December 7th, 1965 to a wonderful couple who loved me unconditionally. I was nicknamed "Peanut" and I am here to tell you how I managed to get a Life Sentence and reveal all the facts of my case.

I pray someone reading this book today will reach out and help me prove I am innocent.

Many are locked away for life and also for a number of years who are just like me, we are wrongfully convicted.

The Orange County Sheriff and Assistance District Attorney say I ran Ms. .... off the road late at night with my girlfriends car.

Then took Ms…………….from her car by "Knife Point" putting her then into my girlfriends car with the intent to violate Ms…………………………. sexually. Then they go on to say, that once I placed her in my girlfriends car Ms…………………… started to fight with me trying to escape the car, but before Ms……………….was able to fight and pull away from me to open the door to escape, that Ms………………..almost lost her leg due to the bad cut to her leg. (This allegedly took place on a very dark and raining night of May30th, 1996.

It's been since 1995 that this nightmare began, but I will do my very best to tell you my statement in details. On or about May30th, 1996 I woke up at my girlfriend's apartment in Clearlake. I guess that would be Houston, Texas. It was around 7 a.m. or a little after when I left to go spend the day with my mother in Vidor, Texas.

My girlfriend had to go to work, so she did not go with me. After leaving her for the day, I went straight to buy some beer; I picked up a 12 pack and went to start my day off. When I got the 12 pack and after drinking 2 or 3 of them as I drove to Clearlake and around to the other side of Houston to Pasading Road. I then went to some apartments where I have bought many times drugs (Cocaine) that I would use through IV use all throughout the day of May 30th, 1996 and into late evening.

I then got on to 1-10 East to go to my mothers in Vidor, Texas. While driving and drinking, I pulled over to different little stores getting off of I-10 east so that I could use their bathrooms for shooting up the cocaine and other times when I didn't go inside the store, I would just shoot up while sitting in my car.

At some point at one of the stores I bought another 12 pack of beer. I also remember having a big hold in my right arm from the same week of IV use. Even though I had this hole in my arm and it was open and bleeding while still shooting cocaine on May 30th, 1996, I would shoot in it and around it, if it was bleeding too much I would wipe it on my left pant leg. At this time I really don't remember the time I got to my mothers, without looking or reading my statement I gave on May 30th, 1996. I do however remembering that with the drinking and shooting cocaine, it took me a really long time to drive from Houston, Texas to Vidor Texas. I believe it was around 11 a.m. or 12 noon by the time I finely got to my mothers.

By this time, I wasn't thinking right. My mind and thoughts were messed up, running wild with thoughts that my mother was going to be pissed and know that I was on something more than just beer. So, when I pulled into my mother's driveway, I got out and opened the gate and then pulled on into the driveway.

Feeling that something bad was going to come out of this visit with my mother just by the shape I was in, I thought at this time I would turn my car around so that I would be heading out, if my mother and I started fighting and arguing, I would say because I would never raise a hand to my mother or dad.

As I was trying to run my car around I found it harder than usual to accomplish. I finally got it turned around and started to back up next to my dad's truck before parking. Without knowing I had cut to close to my dad's truck. I started to scrape or scratch the passenger side of my car against my dad's truck. By the time I could pull up, back up and pull up again, my mother was looking out the window. Before I had got my car right and turned it off my mother was walking outside to meet me. I knew who was pissed and for sure wasn't in the right mind. I got out of my car with a beer in my hand, as she walked up to me.

I gave my mother a big hug, and told her how much I loved her. She was really upset and began telling me things like "You are drunk and look at you, you are on drugs, Peanut you are going to kill yourself or someone driving. I think she tried to take my keys, but I pulled away.

I tried to give my mother another big hug and tell her how much I loved her, but she pulled back, she said something that hurt me I remember and she walked back into the house crying and mad. I was hurting and I was made. I was about to start crying myself and then I looked into the car seat and saw the beer and started thinking how I wanted to drink and shoot some more cocaine. It was then I just got in the care and before I thought I had started driving, thinking I would go to Bridge City, Texas to see and spend some time with my other girlfriend …………. Who was also at this time pregnant with my baby.

On the way from Vicor, Texas to Bridge City, Texas I pulled over to shoot some more cocaine, I was having a hard time being upset and now drinking a lot faster. The needle U-100 I was using got stopped up with blood and dope in it more than a few times, I would take and hit it with my other hand and pushing on it really hard, thus causing blood and cocaine to spray the car in more than a few places.

By the time I got to Bridge City, Texas I pulled into the small trailer park. I was really out of it, my mind just running with so many thought at one time. As I drove to my girlfriend's trailer I saw that there were men and women sitting on their cars at my girlfriend's trailer. I pulled up, shut the car off and got out grabbing my beer to drink.

I heard the radio playing loud music, coming from the trailer. I leaned up against my car.. Looking around I knew everyone by face but not name. I only knew about one or two of them. Everyone was drinking, laughing and just having fun. As I stood there drinking I was looking for my girlfriend, she stepped out of the trailer and looked straight at me. We had been arguing the night before because she had wanted me to stop drinking and doing drugs immediately. We had fallen out so bad that she had taken off the rings I had gotten her and said she was leaving me and she went to her sister's trailer, there in the same part.

So on this day of May 30th, 1996 as we stood looking at each other, someone said "Oh Shit" here comes the bitch pulling the in the trailer park, this was the landlord coming. I looked and for some reason I just came off my car and threw my beer towards her and her boyfriend's truck pulling in. I didn't hit their truck, but as she pulled into the first trailer, which was hers I said talking to myself. I better go talk to her in case she gets mad. As I walked to the front of the trailer I saw she had run in her trailer leaving her door open. As I walked toward her trailer I was told by her boyfriend to just stop, that she didn't want to talk to me, that she was in there calling the cops.

With the beer and cocaine pumping me, her boyfriend and I were arguing and then she stepped out of the trailer and said to me "You need to get out of the Trailer Park, I have just called the cops and they are on their way". I told her I was just playing around and that I wasn't really going to hit her truck. She just said "I want you out of the trailer park" I was then so mad that I told her "F.... You" my girlfriend lived here and I was visiting her and I turned and walked back to my girlfriend's trailer. We were all laughing and drinking and jamming to the radio when about 15 to 20 minutes had passed I heard someone say that the cops were coming and they had just pulled in and were talking to the landlord.

Not long before this I had just got out of T.D.C.J. so I grabbed my another beer and was leaning up against the car drinking it when the Orange County Sheriff Department pulled right up next to my car, got out and walked right up to me and said "Mr. Hurst, Mr. John William Hurst?" I said "Yes sir, that's me." "Mr. Hurst how much have you had to drink?" I told him maybe more than enough. He started to laugh and then told me that the landlord said I had thrown a beer at her as she was pulling in almost hitting her. I told him that was a lie, that I did throw one at her but was only playing with her, not trying to hit her truck. "Well she wants you out of the trailer park…Are you driving?" the officer said. I knew better than to tell him yes, because not only was I drinking and high, but I didn't have any driver's license. So I told him "No I was not driving." "Is there someone I can call for you that will come pick you up?" The officer said. I said "Yes my mother."
He then told me, "Mr. Hurst if I take you to that store over there and drop you off and call your mother to come get you, you will

stay there and not walk back over here in the trailer park will you?" "NO, I'll stay at the store until my mother picks me up." So the Sheriff radioed in to the dispatcher and had her call my mother.

I got him to let me sit in the front seat of his cop car and no sooner did he get in the car than the dispatcher came over the radio and told him that my mother and sister would be coming to pick me up. As he was pulling into the store to let me out it started to rain. I got out and walked into the store that would be soon closing, because it was around 7 pm by then.

After the sheriff left, I waited a little bit and when I was sure the Sheriff was gone, I ran into the back of the trailer park and got in my care and left in it. After pulling out of the trailer park, I pulled right into the store parking lot to wait on my mother and sister to show up.

I sat in my car drinking until my mother and sister pulled into the parking lot. The passenger window was half down and stuck so the rain was coming in and the seat of the car was soaked on the passenger side. My mother and sister started talking about which one of them was going to drive my car home.

I told them both I would follow them and that I was driving my own car. Both of them plead with me to let them drive but I said "No". After they saw I was already backing out of the lot, my mother told me to stay behind her and be careful. I told her let's go because the rain was really falling now. As I was following my mother she was just driving too slowly and I was still wired and drinking so I passed her doing about 70 or 80 miles an hour. I lost it two times but somehow brought the car back into control. I got to the house and saw all the power was out and the house door was open. I got out of the car with a beer in hand and set on the hood of the car because the rain I thought would bring me down off this cocaine. The beer just wasn't doing it, no matter how much I drank. I then saw my dad walk out asking "Where is your mother and sister, boy?" I could see and hear he was mad. I told him they should be here soon that I had passed them on the road and she was driving too slowly.

I heard Daddy say something and walk off back inside the house. This took hold on me and hurt because I'm a Daddy's boy. About that time I hear mom and my sister pulling in as they were getting out of the care I jumped up with my arm's wide open to my mother, but she looked at me crying and just side stepped me and walked into the house slamming the door. This being another blow to me that hurt. My sister came and pulled me in her arms and told me to let it go buba and talk with momma and daddy tomorrow, because she said I was in no shape to talk and I was hurting.

I followed my sister to her house next door. I really wanted to run, just get in the car and go, but I walked with my sister to her house and when we stepped in the door the phone rang. She picked it up and walked to her bedroom where her husband was. I heard her say on the phone that I was so messed up, and I then just walked out the door, run to my car and took off once again. I was driving back toward Vidor and I found a beer on the seat. I opened it and started drinking again.

ALCOHOL AND DRUGS HAVE A WAY OF CHANGING OUR PERSONALITY AND THE WAY WE ACT AND THINK.

I found myself back in Vidor so I thought I would go see my wife A.....J.... Hurst. That's right, I had a wife in Vidor, a girlfriend in Clearlake and a pregnant girlfriend in Bridge City.

So I drove through Vidor and went to my wife's home. I knocked on her door wakening her up and she opened the door, saw it was me and asked what was I doing as we didn't live together. I stepped in the doorway, kissing her and told her that I just needed to talk awhile until I could come down off this high. She told me to give her a smoke and I saw that I didn't have any. She asked me to run to the store where she was manager. It was just about two miles back into Vidor, I didn't want to go but I wanted a smoke too now, so I told her to call up there that I would go. As I got back into Vidor and stopped at a red light, I saw two cop cars pull in behind me. As the light turned green I pulled off went under the underpass and hit my blinker to turn right into the parking lot of the store. Both cop cars followed me into the parking lot and then turned on their lights. As I got out of the car both officers walked up to me and one said "Mr. Hurst?" I said "Yes." He then asked me if I would mind taking everything on me and placing it on the back of the car. I asked what was going on and then he said "Mr. Hurst, I don't know what's going on, I was just told to hold you here until someone comes to talk to you. I asked if I was under arrest? He said "Mr. Hurst I got a call to hold you until someone got here and they will be here in a moment, but Mr. Hurst right now I am going to handcuff you and sit you in the back seat of my car. Is anything else on you?" I said "No"

He then placed handcuffs on me behind my back and placed me in the backseat of his car. As I was sitting in his care I saw more and more cops pulling up. Before long the whole parking lot was full of Orange and Vigor Cops. They were walking around my car looking inside every door and window. I could hear officers saying "Yeah, we got him, I see blood all over the inside of the car, yeah he has blood on his pants, boots, Yes there is no doubt about it we got the S.O.B."

Then I saw a plain clothes cop talking to the cop who placed the cuffs on me and put me in his car. I could hear the cop tell the Detective, "Yeh, its him, no doubt he got blood all in the car, on his clothes, yeh, he cut her up f………. good. Then out of no-where two kids about 17, 18, or 19 years of age was banging on the window looking at me yelling and hollering, You Mother F……. you are the one that did that to my sister, you Son of a B……….I'm going to kill you, I know what you look like as they kept on swearing at me and saying "I got you, I know what you look like".

Then the Detective came over slowly and told them, "OK, OK, OK now you've seen him, the best thing you can do is go and be with your sister. You would be helping us if you could just go talk to her and let us do our job here. Then the boys left. After a little bit the Detective opened the door and said, "Mr. Hurst, I need to talk to you. Do you know what I want to talk to you about Mr. Hurst?"

I told the Detective I didn't know just what it was all about but I heard the cops and you talk about blood that's in my car and that's on me and how I cut her up F......good. Then those kids were saying things about me. "Let me tell you Detective the blood you all are seeing in my care and on me is from me shooting cocaine all day and my arm has a big hole in it, that's been bleeding a lot."

I showed him my right arm and told him "Any blood in that car and on me is my own blood. I may not have O.J.'s money but you can do DNA testing on all of it, my car, my clothes, me whatever. I haven't cut no girl up, you hear me?"

The Detective asked me would I sign something to let them look in my car and then go to the station with me and write a statement to what I have done since I woke up that day.

I told him "Hell Yes, what you want me to sign? Where's it at? I'm not under arrest am I?' He said "No", so I signed my car over to them and when the Detective and I got to the Orange County Department, I signed over my clothes .. all of them.. my boots and knife that I had on my side etc. Everything.

Once I gave my statement and signed it then the Detective and his partner gave me a ride to my mother's house on May 31st, 1996 about 7:30 a.m.

(1) I feel if the DA of Orange County hadn't told the Judge when he asked why was there no D.N.A. testing done? The DA said "Due to Orange county Budget we felt no need to go for D.N.A. Test. Both E.D........ and myself turned out to have A+ blood. Forensic A.F. who tested hairs, blood, clothes, said that she could only say there was "Similar" But only with D.N.A. testing could it be for sure whose blood it was. After I had already been in T.D.C.J. for 9 years, a

new D.N.A. Law was passed I myself had D.N.A. testing done on all evidence used to convict me by the "Public Safety Crime Laboratory Service, Austin Texas, Case No. L-330663. When test was completed March 2nd, 2005 – Test EXCLUDED the victim, E. D…….. and furthermore all testing made me "John William Hurst" as being the donor of all blood to D.N.A. testing. I believe that if the Jury would have heard this evidence, I would not be here today. Because if I would have cut her leg, right hand so bad while she was fighting and tying to exit the car there would have been blood from her on the floor of the car, seat and door. BUT there was none.

(2) Forensic Chemist, D….. S…… stated paint chips were "Similar", and that the paint chips could have come from any batch of paint or from a lot of cars.

(3) I believe that the only way the victim, E….D….. was able to pick me from a "Picture Line Up" was because of her brother who ran up on the cop car and his friend told her which One of the pictures they saw in the cop car.

(4) The I.D> Card that the victims dad
and brother claimed to have found at
the crime scene 3 or 4 days later and
didn't turn it in to D.T. until after a
week had past, if that was my
daughter and I found an I.D. Card
that belonged to the girlfriend of the
man that was supposed to have done
something to my daughter I would
have turned it in the same time I
found it .. Wouldn't you? There were
some Orange police officers who went
to my girlfriend H……. in Bridge City,
Texas trailer and while no one was
home searched her trailer. The
landlord let them in without a
warrant. The reason for this search
was never clarified. Then days later
my girlfriends Texas I.D. card along
with a pair of sandals that belonged
to the victim was found neatly beside
each other by the victim's father.
But, he never turned it in until after a
week later. I believe this was all
PLANTED EVIDENCE, by Orange Cops
or my pregnant girlfriend who was
mad at me.

(5) The only reason I was convicted of this
crime was because I was convicted of

rape at the age of 16 in 1983 and Vidor and Orange County Officers did not want me in Orange County.

(6) I believe that if my attorney would have let me on the stand to tell my side myself, the Jury would have gotten a better understanding. But my attorney said he would walk on me if I pushed to get on stand.

LAW ENFORCEMENT INVESTIGATION EVIDENCE

- (A) List the law enforcement agency that investigated the crime and the name of the investigating officers if you know them:
  ORANGE COUNTY TEXAS SHERIFF DEPT. (NAME OF DETECTIVE OF INVESTIGATION? DON'T KNOW)

- (B) How did you become a suspect in the investigation? *BECAUSE OF MY "PRIOR CONVICTION" IN 1983. HER MS.D.......BROTHER AND FRIEND WHO RAN UP ON MY WHILE SITTING IN THE*

COP CAR. I BELIEVE THEY TOLD HER WHICH PICTURE OUT OF THE LINE UP TO CHOOSE FROM (WHICH WAS ME) AS THEY SAW ME IN THE COP CAR, AND THE FACT I WAS ON PAROLE FOR A PRIOR CONVICTION.

- (C) To your knowledge were there any other suspects the police investigated? **NO**

- (D) Why do you think the "Victim" made complaints against you?
BECAUSE OF HER BROTHER AND FRIEND TELLING HER WHO THE LAW HAD AND THE LAW TELLING HER OF MY PRIOR AND THAT I WAS STILL ON PAROLE.

- (E) When was the first time you spoke with your lawyer? *I TALKED WITH MR. JOE ALFORD, 105 S. MARKET, ORANGE TEXAS, PH.........SHORTLY AFTER HE WAS COURT APPOINTED — JULY 25TH, 1996*

- (F) Did the police or investigating detective ever interview you and how many times were you interviewed?

ONE OR TWO TIMES.

- (G) How long were the interviews? *3 MAYBE 4 HOURS*

- (H) Did you ask for a lawyer during the interviews? *NO*

- (I) Did you sign any papers during the interview and if so, what did you sign? *I SIGNED MY STATEMENT AND THE PAPERS TO TURN MY CAR AND CLOTHES, BOOKS AND KNIFE TO INVESTIGATING OFFICER FOR ORANGE SHERIFF'S DEPT.*

- (J) Did you give a confession to investigating officer? *NO*

- (K) Did you make a statement, if yes why? *CAUSE I KNEW I HADN'T DONE ANYTHING AND I JUST WANTED TO GO HOME TO GO TO SLEEP*

- (L) Did you sign the statement? *YES*

- (M) Was the statement admitted in trial? *YES*

- (N) Please list the names of all alleged victims of offense which you were convicted: *Ms. E. D..............*

- (O) Did any eyewitnesses identify you and if so when and where? *ONLY MS. E. D.......... BY PHOTO LINE- UP WHILE IN HOSPITAL AND IN COURT.*

- (P) Did anyone else identify or implicate you? *YES, MS. D.......... AND HER BROTHER AND HIS FRIEND IMPLICATED ME WHEN HER BROTHER SAID "YOU'RE THE ONE THAT DID THIS TO MY SISTER... MOTHER F....... I'M GONNA KILL YOU".*

- (Q) If someone identified you, specify who it was and whether they testified. *E. D.........AND SHE TESTIFIED IN COURT.*

COURT PROCEEDINGS

(A) PRE-TRIAL

1. Were you offered a plea? Yes what was it? 105 Years.
2. Did you take the plea agreement? No..
3. Why or why not? I was not guilty.
4. What was your final plea? Not Guilty.
5. Name, address and phone number of trial lawyer? Joe Alford,

   ....
   ....
6. Name, address and phone number of any investigating officers? Don't know without court records.
7. Name of the prosecuting District Attorney? John Kimbrough, Asst. District Attorney, Orange County, Texas.
8. Name of the Judge presiding in your case? Judge Buddie J. Hahn, 260th Judicial District, Orange County Courthouse, Orange Texas.

(B) TRIAL INFORMATION

1. Did you testify? NO   Why Not?
   Because Attorney said he would
   walk off my case if I tried to push
   to get on stand. Because I wanted
   to tell my side.
2. Did the Victim Testify? YES
3. Did any surviving family member
   or friend give a victim impact
   statement? Yes Victims mother,
   dad, brother and friend. Don't
   know names without court records.
4. List the witnesses that testified for
   the STATE, how they are related to
   the case and briefly describe the
   testimony of each witness? Mrs. &
   Mr. D……….. Brother, sister, friend.
   Also lady from my prior conviction
   and a past school teacher from my
   past who all had nothing good to
   say about me. – Need court record
   for name and brief testimony.
5. Did any expert testify for the
   STATE and what kind of expert
   testified, address and phone
   number? Forensic Angela
   Fitzwater, stated that she could
   only say that the testing for the

blood, hair and clothes was SIMILAR. That without DNA testing nothing could be said for sure…. Forensic Chemist, stated that he could only say that the paint chips were SIMILAR… but also that the paint chips could have come from a lot of cars and trucks. For phone numbers and addresses they will be found in court records.

6. List the witnesses that testified for the DEFENSE. How they are related to the case and briefly describe the testimony of each witness? My mother, dad, sister, brother in law and wife. All gave testimony in court as to the written statement I gave on my behalf of what happened on May 30th, 1996.

7. Did any expert testify for the defense? NO

(C) EVIDENCE
(Answer even if you take a plea)

1. Physical Evidence/Non Biological, was any recovered? YES

2. If so, please describe: Car, large white envelope with blood on it, all clothing, boots, knife, Texas I.D. Card that belonged to girlfriend (who has now recanted her statement) blood samples and hair samples from me and the victim.

3. Biological Evidence, was any DNA recovered during the investigation of your case? YES
   (A)   Were any bodily fluids or hair samples obtained from the victim and if so, what samples were obtained? YES.. Blood, hair, swabs and clothes that she was wearing the night of May 30th, 1996
   (B)   Were any bodily fluids or hair samples obtained from

you, if so what samples were obtained? Blood, hair, swabs.

(C)   Who took the samples from you and where was it done? The nurse from Orange County Sheriff Dept. and other investigators for the same Dept. Names will be in court records.

(D)   Was any biological evidence found at the scene crime? NO

(E)   Were bodily fluids or hair found on you, your clothing, in your car, home, etc. and if so, what was found? Blood on jeans, blood in car, on my boots, on a white envelope that was found on passenger side of the cares floor board, hair was pulled out of the car, knife on my side and blood on my shirt.

(F)   Was any Biological evidence found on the victim? NO

(G)   Was any testing done on the bodily fluids or hair samples, if yes what kind of

testing was performed?
Yes, just testing to see
what blood type myself and
the victim was.

(H)   Who arranged to have the
testing? The Prosecution.

(I)   Which lab performed the
test? Don't know

(J)   Was testing done on all of
the physical, biological
evidence recovered during
the investigation of your
case? None, other than to
see what blood type was.

(K)   Were the results of the test
used at trial? YES

(L)   Were the results used in
your appeal? No, I don't
think so.

(M)   Please list what items of
evidence you think can be
subjected to a DNA test
and state how that test will
show you are innocent.
The D. A. of Orange Texas
has said he can offer swab
of blood taken from the
passenger door, swab from
the driver's door, white
envelope with blood
splatter that was found in

car and blood cards of blood taken from victim and defendant. Why my car, clothes, boots, knife, hair, can't be offered I do not know. I have never been sent any paper to sign to release or to do away with any evidence. I feel that if DNA testing is done and brought back to court along with other evidence, I will give this time back to the courts.

(N) Have you ever received written notice that evidence in your case has been destroyed? If so, when and from whom? NO none at all..

(C) DIRECT APPEAL

1. Did you or your attorney appeal?
   YES
2. If so, what is that appeal case
   number? NO.09-97-00130-CR
3. If your case still on appeal? NO
4. Name, address, phone number of
   appellate lawyer? Christine R.
   Brown –
   Zeto...

   ....

   ....

(E) PETITION FOR DISCRETIONALY REVIEW (PDR)

1. Did you or your attorney file a
   petition for discretionary review
   (PDR)? I really don't know for
   sure.

(F) WRIT OF HABEAS CORPUS

1. Did you or your attorney file a
   writ of Habeas Corpus in State
   Court? YES
2. If Yes, How many? ONE
3. Name, address and phone
   number of State Writ Lawyer?
   Christine R. B..............

4. For each State Writ filed, list the issues raised, which issues if any did the court decide in your favor?

(1) The trial court abused its discretion in failing to grant appellant motion for mistrial.

(2) The court erred in not including in the Jury charge the request lessor including offense of attempted agg. Sexual assault.

(3) The appellant was not granted effective assistance of counsel as provided for in the 6th amendment of the U.S. Constitution. These three issues were brought up in my first appellants brief. As far as my application for a Writ of Habeas Corpus, 11.07 filed 2/14/2006 case No. D460354.

(1) Actual innocence Demonstrated as a result of DNA testing of evidence not

available at time of trial. Defendant requested defense council to DNA test blood evidence and other biological evidence taken from crime scene(defendant's car) and was told by counsel that state could not afford DNA test for indigent defendants. Pursuant to Article 64 Texas code of criminal Proc. Motion DNA testing of said evidence revealed that complainant could not have been physically inside defendant's car and thus complainant's story is not supported by the physical and scientific evidence taken from scene.

(2) In effective assistance of counsel had defense counsel actually had DNA testing conducted on the states biological evidence recovered from defendants car (the crime scene) such evidence when presented to the jury very easily could have swayed Jury into a verdict of acquittal, especially in light of police conducting a warrantless search of defendants home at which, defendant maintained police secured defendants girlfriends State I.D. card and sandals which were conveniently found at place of alleged offense. The jury was entitled to hear this evidence.

(3) Warrantless search and seizure produced evidence which should not have been introduced at trial. Investigators had defendants landlord open defendant's home for search of premises which resulted in critical evidence being seized and planted by police at the location of alleged offence, allegedly showing defendant's guilt. Without this evidence, the Jury may very well have voted for acquittal.

(4) Did you/your attorney file a writ of habeas corpus in FEDERAL Court? NO

VI. CASE MATERIALS
Materials I have available for you.
Laboratory reports/direct appeals brief- state and petitioner/habeas corpus writs, 11.07 DNA motions and findings.

OTHERS..
Caption:
Clerk's record and clerk's summary sheet, clerks final certification 4/21/2006
Criminal docket (writ) case no. D960354AR, Application for writ of habeas corpus 3/24/2006

Waiver of certified mail notice 3/27/2006
Notifying writ filed 3/27/2006
Findings of Fact 4/4/2006
Clerk Final Certification 4/21/2006
Original docket sheet D960354-R
Indictment 7/10/1996
Mandate 4/12/1999
Judgment and sentence

These are some of the events of John William Hurst's case from 1996. He has been incarcerated and seeking help from anyone who will listen and take an interest.

Contact John @

John William Hurst 786971
Telford Unit
3899 State Hwy 98
New Boston, Texas
75570

Contact Rev. Anne Skinner @

Prison Letters,
MPO Box 2813,
Niagara Falls, New York
14302

Email: hannahhouse2002@gmail.com

Website: http://hannahhouse2002.org

HARD TIME

It's waiting on letters, when doing your time
And your people won't write or send you a dime.
It's waiting on visits that never take place
From friends or loved ones
Who've forgotten your face?
Its hearing them lie and say that they're trying
Making you promises, but you know they're lying.
It's making plans with someone you thought you
knew,
But their plans suddenly changed and they didn't
include you.
Its hearing them promise and it goes straight to your
heart,
But when push comes to shove they leave you for
dead.
It's the feeling of Love, Honor and Pride,
Pain and Emotions Hurting inside.
It's expressing yourself to your loved ones and friends,
But they can't feel your pain because you're in the Pen
It's really messed up when you're doing time
But that's Prison life:
Out of sight, Out of mind!

By John William Hurst 201

Books can be purchased at
Amazon.com

http://hannahhouse2002.org